Instrumental Solos for **CLARINET**

RODGERS AND HAMMERSTEIN™

How To Use The CD Accompaniment:
A melody cue appears on the right channel only. If your CD player has a balance adjustment,
you can adjust the volume of the melody by turning down the right channel.

ISBN 0-634-02724-7

A RODGERS AND HAMMERSTEIN COMPANY
www.williamsonmusic.com

EXCLUSIVELY DISTRIBUTED BY

CORPORATION

7777 W. BLUEMOUND RD. P.O. BOX 13819 MILWAUKEE, WI 53213

Visit Hal Leonard Online at
www.halleonard.com

The offering of this publication for sale is not to be construed as authorization for the performance of any material contained herein.
Applications for the right to perform THE SOUND OF MUSIC, in whole or in part, could be addressed to
The Rodgers & Hammerstein Theatre Library
229 West 28th Street, 11th Floor
New York, NY 10001
Tel: 800/400.8160 or 212/564.400 • Fax: 212/268.1245.
E-mail: theatre@rnh.com • Website: www.rnh.com

RODGERS AND HAMMERSTEIN™

THE SOUND OF MUSIC®

Contents

	Page	Track
Do-Re-Mi	3	1
The Sound Of Music	4	2
Maria	5	3
My Favorite Things	6	4
Edelweiss	7	5
The Lonely Goatherd	8	6
Sixteen Going On Seventeen	9	7
So Long, Farewell	10	8
Climb Ev'ry Mountain	11	9
"B♭" Tuning Notes		10

◆ DO-RE-MI

CLARINET

Lyrics by OSCAR HAMMERSTEIN II
Music by RICHARD RODGERS

❷ THE SOUND OF MUSIC

Clarinet

Lyrics by OSCAR HAMMERSTEIN II
Music by RICHARD RODGERS

❸ MARIA

CLARINET

Lyrics by OSCAR HAMMERSTEIN II
Music by RICHARD RODGERS

◆ MY FAVORITE THINGS

CLARINET

Lyrics by OSCAR HAMMERSTEIN II
Music by RICHARD RODGERS

◆ EDELWEISS

Clarinet

Lyrics by OSCAR HAMMERSTEIN II
Music by RICHARD RODGERS

◆ THE LONELY GOATHERD

CLARINET

Lyrics by OSCAR HAMMERSTEIN II
Music by RICHARD RODGERS

◆7 SIXTEEN GOING ON SEVENTEEN

Clarinet

Lyrics by OSCAR HAMMERSTEIN II
Music by RICHARD RODGERS

Relaxed Soft Shoe

Piano/Strings

◆8 SO LONG, FAREWELL

CLARINET

Lyrics by OSCAR HAMMERSTEIN II
Music by RICHARD RODGERS